Elder Care Services
Starting and Managing a Profitable Senior Care Business

Table of Contents

Chapter 1. Introduction

In this riveting Special Report, "Elder Care Services: Starting and Managing a Profitable Senior Care Business," we spotlight a major business trend in tune with the times - services for the rapidly growing senior population. A venture teeming with challenges, yet abundant with opportunities. Forget the humdrum business ventures, this report explores an industry primed for compassionate individuals with an entrepreneurial spirit, revealing how to start, manage, and ultimately profit from a business in elder care services. With practical advice, tried-and-tested tactics, and stores of inspiration, this report is designed as a catalyst, ready to spark your entrepreneurial journey. Make sure to get your hands on a copy, and treat yourself to knowledge that could illuminate a potentially lucrative path forward with deep societal significance!

Chapter 2. The Emerging Market of Elder Care Services

The world population is aging at an unprecedented rate. According to the United Nations, the number of people aged 60 years or over is projected to double by 2050, surpassing 2.1 billion individuals. The magnitude of this demographic shift has significant repercussions on numerous facets of our society, particularly in regards to caring for this aging population. This transformative trend that extends beyond borders and cultures presents both challenges and opportunities, and it is in this light that the business of elder care services emerges as a market of the future.

2.1. Elder Care Services: A Snapshot

Elder care services encompass a wide array of services designed to assist and support the elderly in their daily activities and medical needs. These services range from home care (assisting with tasks such as cooking, cleaning, shopping, and personal hygiene), to different forms of community care (daycare centers, group homes), and extensive health care (hospitals, assisted living facilities, nursing homes).

What ignites the need for these services is the understanding that as people age, they often require additional support. Aging is associated with numerous challenges – declining health, decreased mobility, sensory impairments, cognitive decline. Thus, the elderly population becomes heavily reliant on assistance, whether to help with basic daily tasks, provide medical care, or simply offer companionship.

2.2. Market Dynamics

The elder care services market is primarily driven by the expanding elderly population. Statistics indicate that the proportion of senior citizens in total global population has been increasing steadily. With medical advancements leading to longer life expectancies, this trend is projected to continue.

Moreover, the nature of modern societies plays a key role in fueling the demand. Changes in family structure, such as smaller, more nuclear families, coupled with high rates of mobility, often mean that older adults may be left to live alone. Women, traditionally the primary caregivers, are also increasingly partaking in the workforce, leading to what's known as the 'caregiver gap'.

Widespread changes in public policy and legislation are further pushing the demand for elder care services. Many countries are recognizing the needs for taking care of their aging populations, resulting in policy changes that are encouraging the growth of professionally managed elder care services.

2.3. Spotlight on Opportunities

The rapidly escalating global senior population presents extraordinary market potential for businesses within the elder care services sector. Here are a few compelling opportunities:

1. Personalized Care: As elder care services continue to evolve, there's a growing demand for personalized and specialized services, from physical therapy to memory care for dementia patients.

2. Technology Integration: The integration of technology into the elder care industry opens myriad avenues for innovation. From digital health monitors to assistive robots, the senior care tech market is booming.

3. Staffing Solutions: Given the rising demand for caregivers and the ever-present shortage, businesses focusing on staffing solutions may find considerable opportunities.

4. Infrastructure Development: The need for senior-friendly infrastructures, from home modifications to assisted living facilities and retirement communities, is continually on the rise.

2.4. Navigating the Challenges

Success in the elder care services market is not without its share of challenges.

1. Workforce Issues: Recruiting, training, and retaining competent staff in the elder care services industry can be challenging. Caregiving is a physically and emotionally demanding job that often comes with low pay and high stress.

2. Regulatory Compliance: Staying up-to-date with current regulations, policies, and guidelines around elder care services in your area is crucial, as is ensuring the business complies with these requirements.

3. Customer Trust and Satisfaction: Building trust in this sector is enormously important. Negative experiences can have severe consequences. Hence, ensuring quality care and customer satisfaction remains a top priority.

4. Financial Constraints: Pricing services in a way that covers costs, attracts clients, and generates profit can be difficult. Furthermore, potential economic downturns and changing governmental funding can greatly impact operational stability.

2.5. Starting & Managing a Profitable Elder Care Business

Into this field of challenges and opportunities, the question arises - how does one start, manage, and ultimately profit from a venture in elder care services?

1. Business Plan: As with any business venture, creating a comprehensive business plan is vital. This should cover details about your target market, the services you plan to offer, a thorough competitive analysis, and a financial plan.

2. Licensing: Depending on the jurisdiction, you may need to obtain special licenses or certifications to operate an elder care service. Do your research and ensure all regulations are met.

3. Staffing: Hiring the right team and offering them consistent training and education is critical. Remember, it is your staff who will be directly interacting with your clients.

4. Quality of Care: It's essential to establish a standard of care that reinforces a strong reputation for your business. Regular quality checks and feedback sessions can help maintain high standards of service.

5. Marketing: An effective marketing strategy can be the difference between a flourishing business and a failing one. Use a combination of online and offline techniques to reach your target audience.

With diligence, perseverance, and the right approach, a profitable venture in this field could very well be within reach. There's much work to be done, but the potential for financial success - not to mention the chance to make profoundly positive contributions to individuals' lives and society at large - is vast and compelling. It's a sector ripe for compassionate innovators with the business acumen to cast a vision, rally a team, and diligently serve the needs of an ever-growing market.

Chapter 3. Identifying Your Target Audience in Senior Care

Understanding your target audience is a critical first step to setting up a successful elder care business. The senior care market is vast and varied, with different groups of seniors requiring different types of services. You need to identify and understand the needs and preferences of your target audience. This will allow you to build a business that provides solutions to specific problems and meet their needs in a way that no other business does.

3.1. Demographics and Psychographics

Determining the demographics of your potential clients include factors such as age, gender, income, race and ethnicity, marital status, geographical location, and level of education. Psychographics, on the other hand, focus on personal attitudes, values, and lifestyles.

Older adults aren't a monolithic group, so it would be ineffective to market your services to all seniors in the same way. Knowing their demographic and psychographic details can guide you in developing a business model, selecting services, forming marketing strategies, and setting competitive pricing.

3.2. How to Gather Data

Getting to know your target audience can be done in various ways, including conducting online research, surveys, one-on-one interviews, and focus groups. Market research reports and census data can also provide a wealth of demographic information.

Surveys and interviews help gain insight into the psychographics of your target audience. Consider collaborating with local community centers, senior centers, or health care professionals who interact with older adults frequently. They can facilitate connections and help you gather valuable insights.

3.3. Understanding Market Segments

In the senior care business, four main segments cater to different needs and wants: home health care, residential care, specialized care, and companion care.

Home health care serves seniors who need medical assistance but wish to stay at home. Residential care includes retirement homes, assisted living facilities, and nursing homes. Specialized care is for seniors with particular conditions, such as memory loss or mobility issues, while companion care provides seniors with company and help with daily tasks, without medical involvement.

Study these segments carefully to identify where your services would fit best. Each segment has different client profiles, pricing models, and requires distinct staff skills and training.

3.4. Differentiating Your Services

Once you've gathered data and understood the market segments, it's time to align your services accordingly. Differentiating your services can make your business stand out in a crowded market.

For instance, if your target audience consists of seniors with high disposable income who value independence, you might specialize in high-end home health care, providing services that most home health care businesses don't offer, like physical therapy, nutrition counseling, and more.

If you're catering specifically to clients in a geographic locale, you might modify your services to better suit the specific cultural or societal preferences in your local area.

Remember, being everything to everyone is not a viable or effective strategy, so focus on a niche that aligns best with your business plan, mission, and vision.

3.5. Changing Needs and Trends

As seniors age, their needs and preferences may change, often moving from one segment to another. Stay updated on trends in the elder care industry. Keep tabs on the changes in laws, medical advancements, or technology developments related to senior care. These insights will help you pivot or adapt your services to meet changing needs and trends.

3.6. Making an Emotional Connection

The decision to seek elder care usually involves a high degree of emotion – both for seniors and their loved ones. Understand this emotional journey. Empathize with your clients' emotions, build trust and establish a solid relationship. Your business should not only cater to the practical needs but also engender feelings of security, comfort, caring, and positivity.

In conclusion, identifying your target audience in senior care is not just about recognizing who needs your service. It's about understanding their specific needs, preferences, the emotional journey they're on, and acting accordingly. By doing so, you can better align your business offering, helping your clients lead a more comfortable life and making your business a successful and profitable venture.

Chapter 4. Crafting Your Business Plan for Elder Care Services

Beginning the journey into the world of elder care services business demands a solid, well-planned outline aptly known as your business plan. This foundation is what shapes your future activities, goals, and venture strategy. The business plan covers various aspects of your operations ranging from the business model, marketing strategy, financial projections, and much more. It is the roadmap that guides your venture and gives potential investors an overview of what you envision your elder care services to be.

4.1. Defining Your Vision and Mission

Your business plan must start with the establishment of your mission and vision statements. These key elements communicate your business purpose and the goals you aim to achieve. Your mission statement embodies your company's philosophy and outlines the firm's reason for existing. Your vision statement expresses your company's long-term aspiration.

Ensure that your vision and mission are crafted to mirror the essence of your elder care services. The senior care industry is centered around offering exceptional care to the elderly. Hence, your statements should reflect empathy, care, and the desire to improve seniors' lives.

4.2. Business Model

The next step in crafting your business plan revolves around your business model. This describes how and where you'll offer your elder care services. Will it be a home care service where caregivers visit customers at home, or will it be a residential facility? Who is your target market? And more importantly, what are the specific services you're offering?

These are significant considerations that influence your day-to-day operations, revenue streams, and cost structures. Incorporate a detailed analysis of these components in your business plan, justifying each aspect with market research findings and business logic.

4.3. Market Analysis

To showcase that your venture isn't a shot in the dark, a section of the business plan should be dedicated to a complete market analysis. Enumerate and describe your target demographic, their needs, and how your services meet these needs. Gather information about the size and growth projections of the local elder care services market.

Identify your competitors, their strengths and weaknesses, and how you'll differentiate your services. This competitive analysis will equip you to focus on specific areas that guarantee customer satisfaction and attract clientele from rivals.

4.4. Marketing and Sales Strategy

Arguably, one of the most critical sections of your business plan is the marketing and sales strategy. It's the framework through which your services become visible to potential clients and their families. This section delineates how you'll attract your target market to your services.

Your marketing strategy could include tactics like community healthcare events, partnerships with local hospitals and doctors, an engaging social media strategy, and more. Detailed sales strategy encompasses understanding customer needs, building customer relationships, and offering value.

4.5. Operations and Management

Proceed to describe in detail how you'll go about the day-to-day operations of your elder care business. Highlight the staffing requirements, typical daily schedules, care quality assurance checks, and training programs. This part of your business plan also explains your management structure, showing who will be in charge of which aspects of your operation.

4.6. Finances

Before launching your elder care service, understanding its financial dimension is paramount. The financial section of your business plan covers your startup costs, the operating costs, projected income, and profitability timeline.

Draw up detailed financial projections for the next three to five years, including balance sheets, cash flow statements, and profit and loss accounts. It helps assess financial sustainability and determine future funding needs.

4.7. Risk Assessment

Every entrepreneurial venture comes with its own set of risks and hurdles. Incorporating a risk assessment within your business plan presents a clear picture of your anticipation and preparedness for potential challenges. Hence, identify possible risks like regulatory changes, staff turnover, or market shifts, and detail out your mitigation strategies.

A comprehensive and well-detailed business plan is your launchpad into the elder care services sector. It is not only for lenders and investors but also an indispensable tool for yourself. You get to understand the depth of what you're diving into, making you better prepared and equipped to serve the market needs efficiently. It's a living document that should be revisited and revised periodically as your business evolves with time. Above all, your business plan is a blueprint for your success in the passionate world of elder care. One that is hued in empathy, high-quality care, and business robustness. It's where compassion meets enterprising spirit.

Chapter 5. Essential Licenses and Certifications

Starting a senior care service is not an enterprise that can be launched on just goodwill and financial resources. It also demands sound legal and professional knowledge. This involves obtaining and maintaining the appropriate licenses and certifications, which are vitally important to establish and run such a business efficiently and ethically.

5.1. How Licenses and Certifications Play a Role

When you're ready to take the first step towards commencing a senior care business, there are initially mandatory licenses and certifications to obtain. These credentials, unlike general business licenses, are issued by state and/or the federal government and specifically pertain to health care services. They serve as proof of responsibility and skill, validating your ability to run the elder care services business. Overall, having these licenses and certifications create trust, forms a legal ground for your business operations and ensures that the care provided meets regulatory standards.

5.2. Understanding the Different Categories

Knowing the various types of licenses (such as home health care, nursing home, and assisted living facility licenses) and certifications required is key in deciding the services to provide. Now, while these types differ somewhat across states, there is still a general consensus regarding their requirements.

5.2.1. Home Health Care License

A Home Health Care agency delivers medical services at the patient's home. Before applying for the license, agencies must fulfill several prerequisites. Agencies must employ a registered nurse as a supervisor, provide skilled nursing services, and offer at least another therapeutic service such as physical, occupational, or speech therapy, medical social services or home health aide services.

Moreover, application for this license necessitates a detailed description of the operational plan including hiring protocols, care provisions, safety measures, and contingency plans. The agency should also have a civil rights compliance assurance in place and demonstrate proof of adequate financing to run the agency.

5.2.2. Nursing Home License

Running a nursing home requires the acquisition of a Nursing Home License. Prerequisites to obtain this license include a suitable facility to house residents, an efficient staffing plan including at least one full-time registered nurse, evidence of sufficient financing, and a comprehensive plan for the services provided, which includes nursing care, pharmaceutical services, rehab therapies, and other specialized services such as dental and podiatric services. To renew the license annually, nursing homes must be inspected to ascertain it adheres to safety, health, and care standards.

5.2.3. Assisted Living Facility License

For starting an Assisted Living Facility, you need to obtain an Assisted Living Facility License. This license asks for proof of the facility's appropriateness, demonstration of adequate staff along with their qualifications, necessity of a detailed service plan which includes personal care, supportive services, and health-related services, and financial viability. Maintaining this license requires periodic inspections of the facility to ensure adherence to regulations.

Depending on the state, there may be other categories of licenses as well like an Adult Day Care License or a Residential Care Facility License. Understand each of these requirements in detail and identify which license aligns most with your business model.

5.3. The Role of Certifications

Certificates are another form of proof of your commitment to providing quality care. They act as a symbol of recognition for mastering certain skills and affirm your capability in managing a senior care business. From a Certified Senior Advisor (CSA) to a Certified Nursing Assistant (CNA), different certifications can bolster your mastery in the industry and build credibility.

5.4. The Course of Application

After you have decided the licenses and certificates needed, you must gather relevant documents and fill out an application form (online in most states). Then, pay the application license fee, which may differ by the type of license and the state where you are starting your business. Post this, the agency will review your application, and if approved, issue your license.

5.5. Preparing for Surveys and Inspections

Upon receiving your application, most states conduct onsite surveys or inspections to ensure your facility or agency meets the standards and is ready to start. These inspections are usually unannounced and periodic to ensure continuous compliance with rules, assess the quality of care, and confirm the safety of residents.

5.6. Keeping up with License Renewals and Continuing Education

It's equally important to keep tabs on the due date for your license renewal and ensure it doesn't lapse. Penalties for lapses could include hefty fines, or worse, shutting down your business. Most states also mandate continual education or training to renew licenses or maintain certifications.

5.7. Adapting to Change: Policies and Regulations

Health care policies can change, given shifts in societal values and government provisions. As an elder care business holder, it's crucial to stay informed with current regulations and policies to maintain compliance.

Starting an elder care service business demands dedication, hard work, and unwavering commitment, not only towards your goal but also in meeting the strict yet indispensable licenses and certifications requirements. Remember, it's not about just starting the business, it's also about sustaining it ethically and professionally.

Chapter 6. Staffing Your Senior Care Business: Hiring and Training

Starting your senior care business involves many critical decisions, and perhaps one of the most important is building your team. It's essential that you hire the right individuals for the roles and responsibilities that keep your business up and running. This journey doesn't end after the hiring process - it continues through comprehensive training to ensure top-tier service.

6.1. Identifying the Required Positions

Start by mapping out the organizational structure of your senior care business. This will help you identify key positions and roles you need to fill. Typical positions in a senior care business include business manager, care manager, senior caregivers, and administrative support staff. Each of these roles is essential to smooth operations and the health and well-being of the seniors in your care.

6.2. The Hiring Process

Once you have identified the positions you need to fill, the next step is hiring individuals to assume those roles. Here are some crucial elements to consider during the hiring process:

- Write Clear Job Descriptions: Delineating the responsibilities, qualifications, skills, and experience required for each job will simplify the application and interviewing processes for both you and your candidates.

- Application Review: Look for candidates who have the necessary skills, qualifications, and passion for elder care. Check for certifications and specific experience in senior care whenever applicable.

- Screening and Interviews: A multi-stage interview process that includes phone screenings and in-person interviews can help narrow down your list of prospective candidates. Remember, you're looking for individuals with a special blend of soft skills like empathy and patience, as well as technical competencies.

- Background Checks: Ensuring the safety of your clients is paramount. Conduct background checks on all prospective hires to protect your clients and your business from potential harm.

6.3. Training Your Staff

Employee training is a crucial component of running a successful senior care business. A well-trained staff not only provides high-quality service but also contributes to client satisfaction and business reputation. Here are some key components of an effective training program:

- Orientation: At the beginning of the training process, new employees should undergo an orientation that includes an overview of the organization, role expectations, ethical codes, business values, and culture.

- Technical Skills Training: Offering classes and workshops to sharpen technical skills, such as administering medication, providing basic medical care, or using relevant equipment is critical.

- Soft Skills Training: In the elderly care field, soft skills are equally as important as technical skills. Training programs should emphasize effective communication, empathy, conflict resolution, cultural competency, and problem-solving skills.

- Continuous Training: Continuous training helps keep your employees skillful and updated about the latest in elder care. Offering opportunities for professional development and growth will also motivate your staff, leading to higher retention rates.

6.4. Staff Retention Strategies

Successful staff retention is a result of conscious efforts to create a workplace where employees feel valued and secure. Here are some strategies you could implement:

- Competitive Pay and Benefits: Offering competitive salaries and benefits will help attract qualified candidates and reduce staff turnover.

- Recognition and Rewards: Recognize and reward employees for their hard work, dedication, and achievements.

- Work-Life Balance: Encouraging a healthy work-life balance can lead to happier, more productive employees.

- Professional Development Opportunities: Offering opportunities for continuous learning and advancement can motivate your staff to perform better and stay longer with your organization.

In conclusion, staffing your senior care business effectively requires a multiphase approach. From identifying the right positions to hiring and training skilled candidates, each step builds toward a staff prepared to lend compassionate, high-quality care to the seniors you serve. Successful staffing ultimately impacts client satisfaction, your project's sustainability, and the profitability of your senior care business.

Chapter 7. Marketing Strategies for Your Senior Care Business

Understanding your market and developing effective marketing strategies is key to the success of any business, and elder care services is no exception. With the demographic of 65 years and above projected to double by 2060, the demand for geriatric care services will only continue to increase. To attract this burgeoning market, your business will need to stand out from competitors. This entails a comprehensive strategy tailored specifically for your target audience - seniors and their loved ones - and a deep understanding of their unique needs and preferences.

7.1. Understanding Your Target Market

The first step in any marketing strategy should be understanding who exactly your target market is. In the case of elder care services, your primary target audience likely comprises two distinct groups - the seniors themselves and their adult children or other family members involved in their care.

Consider the seniors' socio-economic status, lifestyle preferences, health conditions, and their families' involvement level and expectations. Similarly, understand the mindset and preferences of the adult children: their financial capabilities, their location relative to the parent, and the nature of their relationship with the parent are all crucial influences on their decision-making.

Conduct market research through surveys, focus groups, and interviews. Take a close look at public health data and national demographics. Understanding your audience will provide the groundwork for your marketing strategies and allow you to deliver a service that matches or supersedes their expectations.

7.2. Positioning Your Business

After thoroughly understanding your target audience, the next step is positioning your business in the market. How you differentiate your business from competitors can be a make-or-break factor.

Identify what unique value you offer - perhaps your facilities have a homely feel, your staff ratio is high, or you offer specific medical care facilities such as dementia care. It could also be your location that is a prime advantage. Whatever your unique selling points (USPs) are, make sure they align with what your target market desires, and then highlight these in your marketing messages.

7.3. Online Marketing

In this digital age, your online presence can often be the first point of contact for potential clients. Your website should be user-friendly, attractive, and informative - optimizing it for mobile devices is also essential.

Ensure that the language used is professional but also resonates with your target audience. Include valuable resources such as blog posts, articles, and e-books on elder care issues. This not only positions your business as a field expert but also boosts your website's search engine ranking, making it easier for potential clients to find you.

Leverage social media platforms where your audience is active. Facebook, for example, is widely used by baby boomers. Use such platforms to share useful content and engage with potential clients.

7.4. Referral Marketing

Strategic partnerships with healthcare providers, hospitals, senior organizations, community centers, and other professional networks can be instrumental in bringing new clients. As trust already exists within these networks, a recommendation can mean a direct line to a new client.

Also, consider launching a referral program, incentivizing current clients or partner organizations to refer new ones. A well-implemented referral program can be a cost-effective way to generate new business.

7.5. Traditional Marketing Methods

While digital marketing is often a central part of any marketing strategy, don't forget about more traditional methods. Direct mail, brochures, flyers, word of mouth, networking events, and local press can be effective at reaching your target audience - particularly seniors who are less connected online and local stakeholders.

Remember, your marketing messages should always focus on the benefits your service provides to seniors and their families. Show how you understand their needs and can help alleviate their stresses and concerns.

7.6. Measuring Success

Monitoring and tracking the results of your marketing efforts is crucial to evaluate their effectiveness. Tools like Google Analytics can track how well your digital ads and website are performing. For traditional marketing methods, you can use questionnaires or direct inquiries to understand which methods are working.

Revision is a critical part of any marketing strategy. Are your ads not yielding the expected results? Then it might be time to revise and optimize them. Is your referral program not taking off? Then reconsider the incentives you're providing or how you're promoting it.

To summarize, a successful marketing strategy for an elder care business revolves around understanding your target market, positioning your business uniquely, leveraging both online and offline marketing methods, creating strategic partnerships, and continuously assessing and refining your approach. It requires efforts on multiple fronts but has the potential to yield significant returns. With time, patience, and execution, you can attract more clients, elevate your care services, and ultimately establish a profitable and sustainable business.

Chapter 8. Financing and Budgeting for Success

The road to establishing a successful elder care business requires a focused approach towards funding its start-up and operational costs. Understanding the nuances of financing and budgeting is therefore essential to sustain and ultimately grow in this industry.

8.1. Raising Startup Capital

Comprehending the financial aspects of starting an elder care business is akin to laying the foundation for a building. Start-up capital is the lifeline that drives the initial phases of the business, and sources for this capital can vary.

One common way to raise funds is through personal savings. Personal savings often serve as the main source of start-up capital for a large number of small businesses. This method doesn't require any third-party involvement or interest fees. However, it involves a significant risk, as you might end up using your life savings.

Another route to consider is seeking capital from friends, family, or private investors. These can offer more flexibility than traditional financial institutions in terms of repayment and interest rates. However, this route brings potential strain to relationships, especially if the business doesn't perform as expected.

Industry-specific grants or government initiatives are another alternative. Various organizations provide grants to stimulate growth in certain sectors. More often than not, these grants are non-dilutive, meaning they do not require giving up any ownership interest in the company. Although competition for such grants is usually intense, securing them can offer substantial benefits.

Bank loans are a common option, but they require strong credit ratings and well-prepared business plans. Banks usually provide loans at lower interest rates than other forms of debt financing but might require some collateral.

8.2. Planning Your Business Budget

Creating an extensive and well-defined budget is critical for every type of business, and elder care is no exception. This financial roadmap guides your spending decisions and aids in achieving short and long-term financial objectives.

Fixed costs in an elder care business are predictable expenses that don't change regardless of the number of clients serviced. This includes rent or mortgage payments, salaries, insurance, and utility bills among others. Understanding these fixed costs helps give a clear picture of the minimum expenses required to keep the business afloat.

Variable costs are expenses that fluctuate based on the number of clients you're servicing. These might include medical supplies, food, and transportation costs. Predicting these costs involves understanding the needs of your client base and then estimating the needed resources.

Revenue projections are crucial components of the budgeting process. These projections should take into account the pricing of your services, the number of clients you plan to serve, and the total hours of care each client requires.

8.3. Cash Flow Management

Maintaining healthy cash flow is essential for the seamless operation of your business. Even profitable businesses can fail if they run out of cash.

Appropriate cash flow management requires regular monitoring of income and expenditure. It means deliberately planning and controlling spending to avoid unexpected shortfalls. It's also important to maintain an emergency fund for unanticipated expenses or to cover costs when the business isn't generating enough revenue.

To maintain positive cash flow, consider offering incentives for early payment to encourage prompt payment from your clients. You can also extend payment terms with suppliers, giving you more time to receive payments before you need to pay your bills.

8.4. Evaluating Profitability

Understanding your company's profitability is essential to making informed business decisions and attracting investors or lenders. There are several key tools for assessing profitability.

The gross profit margin is the percentage of revenue remaining after deducting the cost of goods sold or direct service costs. It provides insights into efficiency and profitability at a fundamental level.

Net profit margin, on the other hand, subtracts all costs, including operating, financing, and tax costs, from the revenue. It provides an overview of your ability to convert revenues into actual profits.

Finally, the return on investment (ROI) measures the efficiency of an investment and provides a ratio that tells the business owner how much profit each dollar of invested money is creating.

Capitalizing on an opportunity like elder care services requires careful financial planning. By raising capital wisely, budgeting effectively, managing cash flow, and evaluating profitability, you can create a successful enterprise with potential for growth that's also providing an essential service to your community.

Chapter 9. Resilience in the Face of Regulatory Challenges

Starting and managing a business in elder care services is not for the faint of heart. It requires tenacity, commitment, and the ability to navigate a sea of regulatory challenges. One may question the worth of facing such difficulties, but the seasoned entrepreneur understands that with great challenges come great opportunities. Understanding, adapting, and growing in response to these regulatory challenges is a vital skill, critical for success.

9.1. Understanding Regulatory Challenges

In elder care services, the first step to effective resilience is understanding the regulatory environment. This sector is heavily governed by rules and guidelines at different levels - federal, state, and local. Legislation such as the Older Americans Act, the Americans with Disabilities Act, Medicaid and Medicare regulations, and the Affordable Care Act all have impacts on the provision of elder care services. Each act has its own requirements, imposing conditions on everything from staffing ratios, building codes, service provisions, to billing processes.

Yet the scope of these rules also varies from state to state, and municipality to municipality. A keen understanding of the rules, compliance requirements, and potential changes within your operating sphere is essential. Regulatory ignorance is not an excuse; it ill prepares businesses for audits and investigations. At best, it invites hefty fines; at worst, it can lead to business closure. Comprehend the guidelines, seek expert advice when in doubt, and never hesitate to ask regulatory bodies for clarifications.

9.2. Adjusting to Changes in Regulations

Next, it is necessary to develop an effective strategy to absorb new regulatory changes. Laws and regulations evolve, becoming more stringent as lessons are leant from previous incidents or as new societal challenges emerge. Whether these alterations occur due to elective changes in political leadership or shifts in societal values, businesses operating in elder care services need to be nimble and readily responsive.

A robust elder care business keeps a vigilant eye on the horizon. Stay up-to-date with legislative debates, participate in industry conferences, or subscribe to regulatory bulletins. Nurture relationships with key stakeholders including government officials, policy formulators, and other industry figures. These relationships can provide early insights into potential changes, allowing for timely modifications to maintain compliance.

9.3. Building Regulatory Compliance into Operations

Building a business model resilient to regulatory changes does not happen overnight. It takes strategic planning and operational design to make compliance a business-as-usual operation. Part of this planning includes allocation of resources: financial, human, and technical, towards compliance needs.

Consider implementing a compliance department or designating a compliance officer, whose job is ensuring the company remains at par with regulatory standards. Incorporating automated tracking and reporting tools can streamline record-keeping and ease reporting burdens. Never treat compliance as a siloed operation; instead, let it permeate every department of your business, from hiring and training to billing and customer service.

9.4. Turning Regulatory Challenges into Opportunities

Regulations have a habit of seeming like the enemy of business, imposing restrictions and creating operational hurdles. But a smart entrepreneur knows how to interpret rules to their advantage. Regulations often reflect societal expectations and can offer insights into effective business practices that meet these expectations. By forging a path that aligns with these standards, businesses not only maintain compliance but break away from the competition, showing consumers their commitment to care and quality.

9.5. Weathering Audits and Investigations

Audits and investigations are a fact of life in the elder care service industry. Instead of viewing these as threats, see them positively, as opportunities to demonstrate your compliance and commitment to service quality. Prepare for them proactively, maintain orderly records, and train staff on how to handle these situations without panic.

9.6. Fostering Growth in the Face of Regulatory Changes

Resilience in the face of regulatory changes is not just about survival, it's about growth. The ability to prosper, despite an ever-changing regulatory landscape, establishes your credibility and strengthens the business. View each regulatory hurdle as a stepping-stone that takes the business to a new level of growth and success.

In conclusion, regulatory challenges are an undeniable part of operating an elder care service business. Understanding these challenges, adjusting to changes, integrating compliance into operations, and turning challenges into opportunities are key to managing a profitable business in this sector. With these strategies and a resilient mindset, you can not only weather regulatory storms, you can thrive amidst them.

Chapter 10. Customer Service Excellence in Elder Care

Providing excellent customer service is the cornerstone of any successful business, and even more vital in the elder care industry, where the stakes for the clients involved are very high. The empathy, patience, and care required in such services must be emphasized and perfected to make your elder care business flourish.

10.1. Understanding the Importance of Customer Service

A high level of customer service is a must-have in this industry. Elderly people often feel vulnerable, misunderstood and neglected. Their families, too, grapple with stress, concern, insecurity and overwhelm. In many cases, this is their first experience with an elder care service and they would appreciate more than just "service". They seek empathy, comfort, security and trust.

By delivering high-quality customer service, you show your clients that they aren't mere transactions, rather, they matter. Their experiences, comforts, concerns, and satisfaction matter. Each interaction fosters a bond of trust and instils confidence that they're in good hands.

10.2. Hiring Compassionate Staff

Your workforce is, quite literally, the face of your business. Make sure to hire individuals who are not just skilled, but also empathetic and patient. They should be able to listen actively, communicate effectively, de-escalate angry or distressed clients, and deliver tailored solutions.

Staff training should be continuous, encompassing interpersonal skills, communication, assertiveness, stress management, cultural competence, crisis management and more. Additionally, their contributions should be recognized and encouraged to foster a thriving environment.

10.3. Personalizing Your Services

Remember that each client has unique needs, preferences and comfort levels. Providing a 'one size fits all' service would not be appreciated. Instead, aim to tailor your services to each client. This includes tweaking routines, introducing favourite activities, accommodating dietary preferences and more.

Periodic reviews and feedback can help identify areas of improvement and ensure that the services remain aligned with the changing needs and requirements of the elder individual.

10.4. Clear, Timely Communication

Communication is key. Families should be updated regularly about the elder's physical and mental health, activities, dietary changes, and any issues that come up. Create an open channel for discussions, and promptly respond to questions and concerns.

Additionally, ensure your staff communicates effectively with the elder person as well. In times of confusion or conflict, a reassuring word or clear explanation can mean a difference between distress and peace of mind.

10.5. Responsibility and Accountability

In an industry so sensitive, accountability is crucial. Mistakes are human, but your response to them defines your company's repute. Any deviations from agreements or mishaps should be immediately addressed, with heartfelt apologies, honest communication and swift correction.

Also, proactive approach to ensure situations are not repeated displays a strong commitment to service excellence.

10.6. Respect for Elderly Clients

At all times, it is paramount to remember that regardless of age or abilities, each client deserves utmost respect. Having a set of ethical guidelines in place reinforces this, emphasizing that elderly individuals are to be treated with dignity, patience, and consideration.

Rudeness or apathy towards an elderly person can cause immense distress and should not be tolerated. Ensure your staff understands this and brings a respectful attitude to their engagements.

10.7. Implementing Technology

Technology can help enhance service quality. Innovations like electronic health records can help keep track of medical histories and any special needs. GPS devices can ensure safety, whilst online communication platforms can keep families connected.

Yet, important to remember that the technology should be user-friendly, and tech support should be readily available.

In conclusion, an elder care business operates on a different realm compared to other businesses. At its core, it thrives on empathy, compassion, responsibility, personalization, coupled with a high level of customer service. This necessitates prioritizing the welfare and experience of the elderly individuals and ensuring that every action leads to their comfort, safety, and satisfaction. It may be challenging, but also immensely rewarding – a testament to a profession dedicated to serving society's most experienced members with the dignity and respect they've earned.

Chapter 11. Future Prospects: Innovations and Growth in Senior Care

Elder care is no longer limited to the traditional paradigm of retirement homes and assisted living facilities. In the era of technology and a rapidly aging populace, successful business models adaptively morph, simultaneously prioritizing the needs of the elderly and their caregivers. A careful examination of societal trends, technology innovations, and industry growth forecasts can reveal possible trajectories and new opportunities for both budding entrepreneurs and established providers in this sector.

11.1. The Promise of Technology

Innovations in technology have significantly redefined various dimensions of our lives, including the ways we approach elder care. Wearable devices, telemedicine, and smart home technology have already started transforming senior care, enhancing safety, monitoring health, and promoting independent living. These technologies offer myriad opportunities for entrepreneurs to create new services or improve existing ones.

Telehealth services, for instance, are a prime example. According to the American Hospital Association, 76% of U.S. hospitals connect with patients and consulting practitioners at a distance through the use of video and other technology. Companies can design telehealth applications specifically for elderly patients, focusing on user-friendly interfaces, increased font sizes, simplified processes, and features that cater to common elderly health ailments. The rising ubiquity of smartphones and smart devices among the elderly population makes this a potentially profitable arena for innovators.

Artificial Intelligence (AI) is also creating ripples in the elder care sector. AI-powered robots can be trained to perform daily tasks such as house cleaning, cooking, or even making conversations, reducing caregiver burden, and increasing the independence of seniors. Moreover, machine learning algorithms can be used in tandem with wearable technology to predict potential health crises even before symptoms manifest, facilitating early interventions. Entrepreneurs focusing on AI-driven solutions in elder care could undoubtedly ride a high tide.

11.2. The Societal Paradigm Shift

We are witnessing a shift in aging dynamics, with more seniors today desiring to 'age in place'. Providing such services requires a different approach compared to traditional senior care homes. To cater to this shift, there is an increasing market demand for home care services, modifications of home environments to suit seniors' needs, and tools to monitor and assist seniors living independently.

Moreover, with the ongoing COVID-19 pandemic making congregate living environments for seniors less attractive, the demand for at-home personalized solutions is likely to grow even stronger. Business adaptations in this realm could range from doorstep delivery of medical supplies to virtual fitness classes for seniors.

11.3. The Economic Aspect

The senior population is growing faster than any other age group in the U.S. The U.S. Census Bureau forecasts that by 2035, seniors will outnumber children for the first time in U.S. history, with nearly 78 million people over age 65. This growth signifies a rise in potential clients, thereby enlarging the market for elder care services.

At the same time, we see increasing economic independence and wealth among seniors, meaning potential clients have the means to pay for more personalized and high-quality services. Catering to their varied needs requires creativity and innovation. For instance, subscription-based services for engaging recreational activities, tailor-made travel programs, or luxury wellness packages could be profitable areas to explore.

11.4. Transformation through Partnerships and Collaborations

In the age of synergistic partnerships, your business can create a larger impact by partnering with technology firms, medical service providers, real estate firms, or even financial institutions. This could lead to diversified services, development of holistic caregiving solutions, or co-created products for seniors.

For instance, elder care service companies and technology developers could collaborate to design smart homes that consider seniors' safety and wellness. There's also potential in collaborations with financial firms to create innovative financing solutions for seniors, helping them afford the services they require without significant financial stress.

11.5. Preparing a Sustainable Business Model

No matter the exact avenue in elder care pursued, developing a sustainable business model is essential. Profitability comes when efficiency, effectiveness, and scalability align with consumer needs and expectations. Be sure to build in adaptation mechanisms that allow for improvisation with changing demands, technology, and societal norms.

In conclusion, riding the wave requires understanding the demographic trends, acceptance of technological innovations, adapting to societal shifts, keeping an eye on the economic aspects, and fostering partnerships. The elder care sector is brimming with unexplored opportunities waiting to be harnessed by innovative entrepreneurs. With the right execution, this business venture could bring in not just financial gain but also yield significant societal contributions.

www.ingramcontent.com/pod-product-compliance
Lightning Source LLC
Chambersburg PA
CBHW062312290526
45794CB00006B/2775